5 THINGS ANYONE CAN DO TO
HELP THEIR CHURCH GROW

5 THINGS ANYONE CAN DO TO
HELP THEIR CHURCH GROW

PHIL STEVENSON

Indianapolis, Indiana

Copyright © 2007 by Wesleyan Publishing House
Published by Wesleyan Publishing House
Indianapolis, Indiana 46250
Printed in the United States of America

ISBN: 978-0-89827-366-3

All Scripture quotations, unless otherwise indicated, are taken from the *Holy Bible, New Living Translation*, copyright © 1996, 2004. Used by permission of Tyndale House Publishers, Inc., Wheaton, IL 60189 USA. All rights reserved.

All rights reserved. No part of this publication may be reproduced, stored in a retrieval system, or transmitted in any form or by any means—electronic, mechanical, photocopy, recording or any other—except for brief quotations in printed reviews, without the prior written permission of the publisher.

CONTENTS

Introduction 6

1 GET PEOPLE IN 9

2 GET PEOPLE BACK 27

3 GET PEOPLE TO STAY 43

4 GET PEOPLE TO GROW 58

5 GET PEOPLE TO GO 72

Appendix 91

INTRODUCTION

When I was in high school I did yard work for extra income. One of my yard jobs was for a lawyer who had very precise expectations, but he always provided me several options for completing the job he had for me. A typical workday at his home would start with his taking me to the area where he wanted me to invest my labor. He would then tell me what he wanted me to do and explain the various ways I could accomplish the task.

On these occasions, his five-year-old daughter was right there with us. One day he had me pulling weeds and removing many rocks. The daughter, inquisitive as always, had this conversation with her dad:

"Daddy, what's a rock?"
"It is a large stone."

"Daddy, what's a stone?"

"It is a piece of rock bigger than a pebble."

"Daddy, what's a pebble?" This lawyer dad had had enough cross examination. "No more questions, honey," he said. "I have work to do. Do you understand? No more questions!"

To this day, I remember her response. She looked at her dad, her eyes wide with delight, and innocently said, "Why?"

There is power in questions. The right question, asked at the right time, will result in the right progress. Many church leaders simply do not ask questions, or at least, not the correct questions.

The five key areas of this book will be explored by asking and answering five key questions. These questions, asked clearly and answered honestly, will help churches design strategies to more effectively reach their communities and provide a structure for church growth. The questions will help churches flesh out their identity in each of these five critical arenas, while providing a framework for balanced healthy growth.

1. What are you doing to get people *in*?
   (outreach/marketing)

2. What are you doing to get people *back*? (follow-up)
3. What are you doing to get people to *stay*? (assimilation)
4. What are you doing to get people to *grow*? (discipleship)
5. What are you doing to get people to *go*? (becoming missional)

It has been said that knowledge is knowing what to do; wisdom is knowing what to do and doing it. It is my hope that you will take the knowledge you gain from these pages and translate it into wisdom. Apply what you discover to your unique setting and you will find yourself a marvelous partner in God's plan to grow His Church.

GET PEOPLE IN

In a recent Gallup poll it was discovered that the adult unchurched population in America has risen 6 percent over the last twenty-five years to a staggering 47 percent. Ed Stetzer and Dave Putman in their book *Breaking the Missional Code* have observed, "Since 1991, the adult population in the United States has grown by 15%. During that same period, the number of adults who do not attend church has nearly doubled, rising from 39 million to 75 million—a 92% increase."

> North America is the third largest mission field in the world, and the United States is the largest mission field in North America.

These realities inform us that churches must be intentional about reaching their communities. Outreach is not optional for churches that want to be effective. Designing ministry to get the already convinced to attend our churches will not get the job done. We are not the home team any longer—we are on the visitor's field, and the crowd is not with us. Steve Sjogren states it much more clearly and harshly: "We believe that a church that doesn't do outreach is a waste of time."

We need to ask, *What are we doing to get people in?* This is an "outreach/marketing" question. It is designed to get you thinking about ways to effectively connect the unchurched to Christ and a community of believers (your church). It may appear, based on the question's composition, that this is purely about getting folks to come to you; but outreach is much more than simply creating ways to get people to arrive in your doorway. It is about engaging the culture in such a way that the church (body of believers) will be attractive to them. It is the difference between an "attractional" philosophy and an "incarnational" one. (We will deal with this later in chapter five.)

A village beggar was reputed to lack complete mental capacity. Whenever he was offered a choice between a nickel and a dime, he always chose the nickel. After this had gone on for some time, one kind gentleman explained to him, "A dime is worth twice as much as a nickel. From now on, when someone offers you a choice, you should choose the dime."

"Oh," the beggar replied, "I know that a dime is worth more than a nickel. But if I choose the dime, people will stop offering."

This beggar exhibited a wonderful understanding of those he desired to connect with. We need to be just as wise as we attempt to engage people for the Kingdom. If we want to get people to show up at our church we must be wise in our approach. Here are six suggestions to help achieve this end result.

UNDERSTAND YOUR AUDIENCE

George Hunter in his book *How to Reach Secular People* identifies "Ten Characteristics of Secular People." They are as follows:

1. *They are essentially ignorant of basic Christianity.* They are "ignostics"; that is, they are simply ignorant of biblical information. They may have cursory cultural knowledge of Noah, David and Goliath, and so forth—not because of the Bible, but because these stories have crept into the psyche of society.
2. *They are seeking life before death.* They fear extinction more than they seek heaven or fear hell. No longer existing is what is scary, not where they will

be—if anywhere. They are not interested in "fire" insurance (avoiding hell), but "life" assurance (the quality of their life now).

3. *They are conscious of doubt more than guilt.* Guilt is no longer motivating—we have learned to shun responsibility. They doubt much of what the Christian faith offers. The people we engage in our world are in various stages of doubt.

4. *They have a negative image of the Church.* They doubt the intelligence, relevance, and credibility of Christianity, which makes many of them indifferent to the Church. They are interested in what we believe, but what they really want to know is if what we believe makes a difference in our lives and a practical difference in the world.

5. *They have multiple alienations.* They are alienated from neighbors, family, co-workers, and so forth, and this results in incredible loneliness.

6. *They are untrusting.* We need to relate to them as leery or distrustful of our faith, not as evil opponents. It may be that they want to trust, they're just unsure how.

7. *They have low self-esteem.* People struggle with accepting themselves as they are. This makes it difficult to believe anyone else can either.

8. *They experience forces in history as out of control.* Nothing, or no one, is in control. History was out of control, life is out of control, people are out of control. This is reinforced by the disturbing images streamed into their homes daily.
9. *They experience forces in personality as out of control.* Who I am and what I do is out of control. I can't control my family, my friends, or myself.
10. *They cannot find the "door."* People want God, but cannot find God. The door they need doesn't seem available. The door we offer may appear too simple.

In his lecture given at Talbot School of Theology in January 2007, George Hunter augmented his insights to the secular person with observations on postmodern folks. He shared nine characteristics:

1. They assume truth is relative.
2. The do not assume the authority of Scripture or pastors.
3. They are more right brained (creative) than left brained (logical).
4. They are more interested in experience, less in doctrine (their self-understanding is based on "I feel, therefore I am").
5. They expect clarity.

6. They expect relevance.
7. They hunger for community.
8. Their music is their first language.
9. They have shorter attention spans.

These glimpses into the world of the secular and postmodern person can provide us insight into those with whom we want to share the gospel. People will listen, if we share in a way they will understand.

DISTINGUISH EXPOSURE EVENTS FROM EVANGELISTIC EVENTS

Not everything a church does will result in someone coming to Christ. However, most of what a church does should contribute to a person's journey toward a relationship with Christ. People will connect with your church at various points on their spiritual journey. How you engage them at any particular point will contribute to or distract from their moving forward. Rob Toews, former leader of Sol Café of Edmonton, Alberta, Canada, states it this way: "We're a 'coffee stop' or 'information booth' along a spiritual highway." It is vital that you know the role of the event you are doing.

An *exposure* event is designed to let people know who you are. It is a means of making people aware that you are in the community. This could run the gamut from a billboard on the side of a major freeway to a hosted barbecue in the town park.

Copan is a very small Oklahoma town. Jay Friedman started a church there about two years ago. He determined that New Life would be a "church *in* the community, *for* the community." When you turn off the state road into Copan you are greeted by a large billboard that reads "Welcome To Our Community—New Life Wesleyan Church." This is an example of exposure. You are aware of this church and its commitment to the community in which it ministers.

An *evangelistic* event clearly communicates the gospel and gives people the opportunity to respond. Jesus Christ is proclaimed. His salvation message is made available. People know they can choose to walk into a relationship with Him. Often an evangelistic event is coupled with special "linkage" holidays or events such as Easter or Christmas. Or it can be a community-oriented event for which your people have been trained in spiritual conversation. They simply make it a goal to engage people in conversation, trusting the Spirit to open people's hearts.

Super Bowl Sunday has become a national obsession in the United States, if not around the world. It is the largest pizza delivery day of the year. Thousands of people gather in homes to eat, chat, and watch the game. Many followers of Christ will use this as a "Matthew Party," a time to invite their Christian and non-Christian friends to connect around a shared interest—the Super Bowl!

Many churches are beginning to leverage this for an evangelistic event, using DVDs specially developed around football themes, often including well-known athletes sharing their faith in Christ. This opens the door for spiritual conversation and, potentially, an opportunity for people to receive Christ.

Be clear about the type of event your church is providing. This will enable you to define the success of the event according to the desired results. The "success" of an event should not be based on whether or not people come to Christ; a person stepping into a genuine relationship with Jesus is a bonus. I suggest the following success points:

- Exposure event: Did you present the church in a positive light? Do people know where you are if they choose to check you out? Answering yes to both would be success.

- Evangelistic event: Was the gospel presented in a clear, contextualized manner? Were people given the opportunity to respond? Did they know what their response meant? Answering yes to all three would be success.

ESTABLISH A PRIMARY OUTREACH PLAN

What drives your outreach plans? Big events at your church's property? Training and mobilizing your people to share Christ with people in their sphere of influence? A combination of both? Regardless of what you choose, outreach must focus on building relationships. People must personally connect with others. For example, if you have an outreach event at your church, do not depend solely on well-thought-out marketing schemes—the marketing should be a complement to your people extending personal invitations to those they know.

> People want *conversation* more than *conversion*.
> — George Hunter

George Hunter makes the point that people want *conversation* more than *conversion*. They want to connect with others on a personal level. It is when we "do life" together that people are most receptive. When people know we genuinely care, they become interested in what makes us tick. When I served on staff with John Maxwell he would tell us regularly, "People don't care how much you know until they know how much you care." I would paraphrase it in this manner: "People don't care Who you know (Jesus) until they know how much you care for them (personally)."

Our outreach plans must be viewed as what George Hunter describes as "links in a chain." We are only part of the process, but we never know when or if our link will be the one that fastens them to Jesus. I suggest the following be kept in mind as you develop your outreach plan:

- **Connection:** People connect with others on a regular basis in the workplace, neighborhood, and home.
- **Conversation:** In life's journey we share who we are and Whose we are.
- **Community:** We invite people to join us in our communities of faith (church).
- **Conversion:** Somewhere through the fabric of connection, conversation, and community involvement people come to Christ.
- **Commitment:** After their conversion, they are led on a journey toward deeper commitment to the one (Jesus) they have engaged in authentic relationship.

Steve Sjogren reminds us in his book *Community of Kindness*, "We believe the power of God's love is what brings people to Christ—not slick programs, not telling people how bad things are, not evangelism and not theology."

ESTABLISH A REASONABLE CONFIDENCE THAT YOUR EFFORTS WILL BE SUCCESSFUL

The best way to ensure a successful effort is to know your community, determining its unique characteristics. This forces you to move from a programmatic approach to a pragmatic one. You must move away from simply finding a methodology that works for one church in one place and trying to plug it into your "wall socket."

What works one place may not work where you are. Finding out what will work in your particular situation is often the result of trial-and-error learning. Many churches don't like the idea of attempting something unless they are completely sure it will work. There are no guarantees, but the better you know those you want to attract to your church, the more confidence you can have in the strategy you embrace.

A church on the east side of town did an outreach where they gave away free hot dogs. The response was great!

GET PEOPLE IN

Hundreds in their community showed up. They shared the gospel message. People came to Christ. Others liked what they heard and saw; they said they would be back the following week.

A church on the west side of town heard about this and decided they would do the same. They promoted, purchased hot dogs, set up grills in anticipation of a large crowd. No one from the community showed up. In fact, they received a few messages on their church voice mail that were not too encouraging! What happened? Having neglected to research their community, they did not realize that the population had a high percentage of "vegans" (staunch vegetarians).

> You don't have to understand all of culture, but you do need to understand the culture of your community.
> —Ed Stetzer

Here are a few ideas as to how you might learn more about your community:

- Get a demographic study.
- Drive or walk your community and pay attention.
- Do "get-o-graphics"—getting into your community, serving people, and listening to their needs.
- Go to the Chamber of Commerce and inquire about community needs.

- Read the local paper to see what is being reported.
- Go door to door and ask.

DO ALL YOU CAN TO ENSURE YOUR EVENT WILL BE ATTRACTIVE

Any event must be well done. This does not mean it has to be professional, but is must be *quality*—people know if something was done without much thought, and they appreciate it when an effort has been made. Quality can be defined as taking the resources you have and using them effectively.

Service in the community is attractive; it gets people's attention. This is a key area to invest in if you want people to show up at your church. When you are involved in the community, people notice and become interested in who you are.

> Quality is taking the resources you have and using them effectively.

A church in Southern California had done little to participate in their community's life. Each year their city organized a festival, a popular and well-attended civic event. The new pastor of the church went to the business association, who sponsored the event, and asked, "What can we do to help you?" The president of the business association was a bit taken aback. He told the pastor that he'd *never* had a church in their community come to him and ask what they could do to help.

The business leader said they needed people to help manage the parade route, so the pastor mobilized more than seventy people to do this. They were allowed to wear T-shirts with their church name and logo, and the business association even used their church parking lot for the pre-parade staging area. The church's willingness to serve resulted in exposure for them and the potential for people to "show up" at their church in the days and weeks following the event.

> In a *declining* church, typically 1 to 2 percent of its average Sunday attendance is guests from the community; in a *maintaining* church, 3 to 4 percent of its average Sunday attendance is guests from the community; in a *growing* church, 5 percent or more of its average Sunday attendance is guests from the community (Gary McIntosh).

CAPITALIZE ON THE "BEST FRIEND" FACTOR

It has been discovered that when best friends attend the same church,

- They attend more regularly;

- They feel more connected to the church; and
- They feel closer to God and display a more integrated faith.

This being the case, why not leverage it? Put an emphasis on people reaching their friends—especially their best friends. If they insist that their best friend already attends the church, then help them identify their closest friend who is not active in a church.

Here are some suggestions:

- Create opportunities for faith-building friendships.
- Preach a sermon series on the value of friends.
- Schedule a "Lucy and Ethel" or "Fred and Barney" Sunday.

KEY POINTS
- Understand your audience.
- Know the difference between exposure events and evangelistic events.
- Establish a primary outreach plan.
- Ensure the event is attractive to the community.
- Capitalize on best friends.

DISCUSSION QUESTIONS

1. What would you add to this list based on your interaction with others?

2. At your last event, did you present the church in a positive light?

3. Do people know where you are if they choose to check you out?

4. At your last outreach event, was the gospel presented in a clear, contextualized manner? Were people given the opportunity to respond? Did they know what their response meant?

ACTION STEPS

1. Get a demographic study. Drive or walk your community and pay attention. Do "get-o-graphics," getting into your community, serving people, and listening to their needs. Go to the Chamber of Commerce and inquire about community needs. Read the local paper to see what is being reported. Go door to door and ask.

2. List the things you have done this past year to get people to connect with your church. Star (*) the things that have been most effective.

3. List the ways you have advertised your presence to the community. Star (*) the advertising that has been the most effective.

4. Determine the percentage of your Sunday worshipping congregation that are guests from your community.

RESOURCES

- George Hunter—*Radical Outreach*
- Andy Stanley, Reggie Joiner, Lane Jones—*7 Practices of Effective Ministry*
- Lyle E. Schaller—*21 Bridges to the 21st Century*
- John Burke—*No Perfect People*
- Ed Stetzer—*Comeback Churches*
- Chris Conrad—*5 Things Anyone Can Do to Introduce Others to Jesus*

GET PEOPLE BACK

I try to exercise regularly, but doing so can be a bit of a challenge when I'm traveling. Typically when I arrive at a hotel, one of my first questions is "Do you have an exercise room?" During one trip to North Carolina I asked this question and was quickly informed that they did not, but they did have an agreement with a local gym less than three miles from their location. I just needed to go in and let them know I was with the hotel, and I would be given a complimentary pass.

My first visit to the gym I was a bit hesitant. I didn't really believe it would be as easy as the desk clerk had described. I was pleasantly surprised when they welcomed me enthusiastically. I simply had to print and sign my name, and off I went to my workout. It was this ease of entry and the welcoming people that made it easy to return. Honestly, if I had lived in the area, as a result of my experience, I would have joined this gym.

GET PEOPLE BACK

It is one thing to get people to come to your church. It is a completely different challenge to get them back. *What are you doing to get people back?* This is a "critical follow-up" question. I was at a training event in San Diego where the presenter, Gil Sieglitz, shared this statistic: "Only 16 percent of first-time visitors will come back, but 85 percent of visitors who return the next Sunday will stay." This underscores the importance of good follow-up.

> Only 16 percent of first-time visitors will come back, but 85 percent of the visitors who return the next Sunday will stay

Any size church can do excellent follow-up. It is not a size issue, but a relational issue. You don't need a large budget to do follow-up, but you do need a willingness to make the effort. People like to come to a place where they feel welcomed and needed. How well you follow up on visitors will determine, to a great degree, your church's ability to grow.

FOLLOW-UP BEGINS WHEN PEOPLE STEP ONTO YOUR PROPERTY

A church that is serious about follow-up must know when follow-up really begins. And it does not happen sometime after the people leave. Rather, it starts as soon as a person or family sets foot on your property or enters your facility. The gym I used on my North Carolina trip seemed to understand this, as they made sure I was truly welcomed when I first came through their doors. Following are the "Five Fs of the First-Time Visit."

1. First Impressions

This encompasses the parking lot and general outward appearance of the facility. A parking lot does not have to be fancy, but it does have to be clean. Is it easy to get in and out? Are weeds growing out of any cracks in the pavement? Has it been swept recently? If there is striping, is it clear? Or if stripes are not used, what is being used to mark the parking spaces? Are there spaces for people with handicaps? (If not, you are violating the law. Check with your local government to see how many spaces are required for your lot.) Elderly folks? Families with small children? Guests? Are gardens weeded? Are shrubs and trees trimmed? How does the paint look on the exterior of the building? If you have a sign, it is well kept? If it is a message board sign, is the information up to date?

> The entire sum of existence is the magic of being needed by just one person.

2. Friendliness

Most churches perceive themselves as friendly. I have yet to hear a congregation describe themselves as "unfriendly."

However, a church may be friendly to one another, but not too welcoming to new folks.

My friend was on staff at a church he described as very friendly. He had been on staff for about six months when I had the opportunity to visit him. Walking up to the church building I saw some folks talking. They saw me coming, but didn't break their conversation. As I got closer, I initiated a hello. They responded, but again didn't break from their conversation. Entering the building, I saw groups of people chatting. Most gave me brief eye contact, but only one person came over to greet me. A few minutes later, my friend arrived. He began to introduce me around, and that's when the friendliness of the church surfaced. Once I was connected with my friend, lots of people greeted me. I later shared my story with him because I wanted him to be aware that the church didn't necessarily come across as being as friendly as they thought they did.

Gary McIntosh observes that churches can suffer from "fellowship inflammation." This is where only people with certain qualities are let in to the inner fellowship. The church may not even be aware of it, but it exists. In my situation, I evidently needed the connection with someone on the inside to be welcomed at that particular church. Once this was established, I was in! Does your church suffer from fellowship inflammation?

Churches need to be wary of two extremes regarding their friendliness.

First is the church "gauntlet." The gauntlet is set up when a church desires so much to exude a friendly demeanor that they place a gaggle of people at the entry point. One or two genuinely friendly folk can do a great deal to express a friendly atmosphere. An overload of welcoming people, no matter how well intentioned, can be intimidating to first-time guests.

Second is to be overly familiar. There's a difference between being friendly and being familiar. When I visit someplace new I am not ready to tell people everything about me, nor do I want to know everything about them. Too much information, too soon, results in a high level of discomfort. People who welcome others need to learn to express openness without eliciting an expectation of transparency. Consider these opening questions: What

> If guests to our church don't think we're friendly, we aren't.
>
> Gary McIntosh

brings you to our church? How did you find out about us? Is this your home area? Would you like a cup of coffee? Is there anything I can do to assist you?

3. Facility

Every church can have a clean, well-lit, easily accessible facility. It can be attractive in its color schemes. Churches do not have to keep up with all the latest trends in interior design, but they should make an effort to be somewhere in the current decade. I have to tell you, green shag carpet is probably not coming back as soon as you may think. Duct tape repairing seams in carpet does not have the appeal it once did. Mauve and blue wallpaper? Not so attractive any more. Churches need to view their sanctuaries like folks view their living rooms: It is where guests are hosted and spend a great deal of time. Personally, when my wife and I have folks over for the first time, we make sure three areas are ready to go: our entryway, our living room, and our guest bathroom.

The same should be true of churches. The places your guests are most apt to go need to be taken care of very well. These typically include the foyer, sanctuary, nursery, and primary restrooms (especially the ladies'). You need to regularly look at these areas through "first-time guest" eyes. Anyone who has been attending your church less than three months can help here. Ask them what they see in these areas. Try these other suggestions for keeping these areas well maintained:

- Invite a professional child care provider to walk through and look at your children's/nursery areas.
- Ask new moms for nursery suggestions.
- Visit model homes in your area. Observe the color schemes they use.
- Invite an interior designer to offer suggestions for the color scheme in the sanctuary.
- Ask someone in your church who has a nicely decorated home to offer suggestions.
- Take the physical environment seriously. It can do much to enhance the worship experience for everyone. In *Community of Kindness*, Steve Sjogren and Rob Lewin say, "When you are designing the physical environment, your job is to take every single element that the worshiper comes in contact with and to influence that thing as much as possible to have a positive impact on the meeting."

4. Focus

Avoid anything that will focus unnecessary attention on guests at the expense of their privacy. The extreme of this is a church that may ask first-time guests to stand. Or, as happened to me when I was visiting a church, a leader may ask regular attendees to stand, while the new folk remain seated. I became a regular attendee at that moment.

There are other, less obvious, examples. One is wearing nametags. If nametags are used, then everyone should wear one, including the pastoral staff. And don't use different colors to designate guests (for example, green for a guest's nametag; red for all others). They will catch on!

In most cases, taking time to recognize that you have guests will suffice. Give them a general greeting from the platform. Let them know how pleased you are they have *chosen* (key word) to be with you. Inform them of any available information about the church and where they can get it. Many churches will have a kiosk or some other location that guests can drop by for information.

5. Flow and Freedom

This refers to guests' ability to get out of the sanctuary without a sense of obligation to pick up a gift or go to a certain area. People like options. Provide them, and let the individuals decide. I was in a church that let guests know there was a coffee kiosk in the lobby where they could stop by for a cup of coffee and more information if *they* chose.

FOLLOW UP AS QUICKLY AS POSSIBLE

The sooner a guest can be contacted, the better. Preferably, contact should be made within forty-eight hours. However, a contact made the afternoon of their visit is ideal. This contact should *not* be a drop-by visit. I suggest two approaches:

1. A phone call Sunday afternoon. This should be less than a minute, unless the person you are contacting chooses to carry on a conversation. This call is to thank them for investing time in being your guest and to find out if they have any questions. The good news here: Voice mail counts! A sincere message left on voice mail is as meaningful as a person-to-person conversation.

2. A personal note from the pastor. If there are multiple staff, then the lead pastor should write (by hand) a legible and short note. Use printed, half-sheet stationery. Address the note by hand and get it in the mail Monday morning. If the pastor made the call, then the note should reference the call.

PROVIDE A GIFT FOR THEIR HOME

Many churches provide gifts to guests. This needs to be something that is both practical (something they will actually use) and present (it will be in their home for an extended time). Coffee mugs with the church's name have been used frequently. I would suggest including a small package of coffee as well.

One of the most creative gifts I saw was a jar of jam (any brand name will do). The church placed a label with their church information on one side of the jar with the statement "Thanks for jamming us into your schedule." They chose jam because their research indicated that a jam jar the size they used remained in homes an average of three months.

Only your creativity will limit what you do. Consider the following qualifications for an appropriate gift:

- *Make it clever, but not cutesy*. Often we over think an idea. A simple gift that shows thoughtfulness goes a long way in the minds of your guests.
- *Contextualize it to your community*. The gift should be something that makes sense for those in the community in which you minister. What works in another city or across town may not work for you.

- *Change it periodically*. To keep your giving fresh, consider changing the gift every quarter.
- *Include basic information.* Your Web site, service times, and phone number should be obvious.
- *Make it something your members would want, but don't let them have it.* You want this gift special enough that your folks get a bit peeved they don't get it. When your regular attendees begin to wear disguises to get the gift, you know you're on to something.

GIVE GUESTS INSIGHTFUL INFORMATION

The information needs to be such that someone who knows little or nothing about your church can navigate through it. Why? Because it will be given to those who know little or nothing about your church! We tend to forget this basic principle. Here are some helpful hints:

- *Keep the information clutter free.* Include basic information, not all information. If someone looks at the material and it appears "too busy," the person will not bother to read it.
- *Look for "insider" phrases*. Churches love to use acrostics and initials for programs, but they are not welcome in guest material. State clearly what is

what! If someone needs an "insider" lexicon to translate the acrostics, you are in trouble.

- *Don't let people assume.* A good example of this is the youth group. Often churches will want guests to know they have a youth group. But they never clarify what is meant by "youth." What ages are actually considered youth? Even if it is broken down into junior and senior high, this needs to be clarified. Is junior high seventh and eighth grades, or is it middle school (sixth through eighth)? Some even include ninth grade. Don't leave if for guests to assume—you tell them.

- *Contacts should be clear.* If there are people who can be contacted for further information about specific programs or events, make clear who they are and how and when they can be contacted.

- *Drive people to the Web.* Written material cannot adequately communicate everything, so make sure the key areas are covered, and then drive guests to your Web site. The younger or more affluent your congregation or target audience, the more necessary is a Web site. Your Web site should exude quality, include up-to-date information, and be easy to navigate.

ONE LAST THOUGHT

A follow up process is based on getting contact information from your guest. I wish I had a guaranteed method to suggest, but I don't. What I would say is keep in mind what you really want from your guest—you want a way to get in touch with them. All you really need is a name, mailing address, phone number, and email address. What you don't need is side information that you could glean from a phone call or email. The less complicated it is, the more likely your guests will be to actually take the time to give you a way to contact them.

KEY POINTS

1. The Five Fs
   - First impressions
   - Friendliness
   - Facility
   - Focus
   - Flow and freedom

2. Gift Considerations
   - Clever
   - Contextualized
   - Changeable
   - Contains basic information
   - Desired

DISCUSSION QUESTIONS

1. When was the last time you evaluated your nursery and children's areas?

2. When was the last time you updated the interior of your facility?

3. Who might you invite in to provide suggestions for your nursery?

4. Who might you ask to visit a model home and report their observations?

5. How many guests have you had in the last three months?

6. What percentage of those guests have returned?

7. What are you currently doing to follow up with your guests?

8. What are some changes you can make?

ACTION STEP

Review and evaluate your church according to the "Five Fs of the First-Time Visit" chart supplied at the end of this chapter. Be honest in your evaluation. How effective is your church in making people's first visit not be their last?

RESOURCES
- Gary McIntosh, R. Daniel Reeves—*Thriving Churches in the Twenty-first Century*
- Kennon L. Callahan—*Twelve Keys to an Effective Church*
- Steve Sjogren, Rob Lewin—*Community of Kindness*

THE FIVE Fs OF THE FIRST-TIME GUEST

Area	Excellent (1)	Good (2)	Poor (3)
First impressions Steps to improvement:	1	2	3
Friendliness Steps to improvement:	1	2	3
Facility Steps to improvement:	1	2	3
Focus Steps to improvement:	1	2	3
Flow and freedom Steps to improvement:	1	2	3

GET PEOPLE TO STAY

While President John F. Kennedy was visiting the city of San Antonio, he joined the mayor on a visit to the Alamo. He received a special private tour of this marvelous historical site that represents American courage and heroism. The cry of "Remember the Alamo" spurred our young nation on in battle.

Once he completed his tour, a crowd began to gather outside the entrance. Not wanting to face the growing throng, President Kennedy said to the mayor, "Let's leave out the back." Reportedly, the reply he received was, "Mr. President, there is no back door. If there were, we wouldn't have had any heroes."

The back door! It is often viewed as a means of escape. Many church leaders have been enthused by the numbers of folks visiting their churches. It seems they see new faces each week. But they are discouraged by how few they keep. Their discouragement is expressed through phrases such as

- "We need to do a better job of closing the back door";
- "We have a big back door"; and
- "Our back door seems to be getting wider and wider."

This challenge brings us to our third question: *What are we doing to get people to stay?* This is an "assimilation" question. It addresses the need for churches to design an intentional methodology to get people connected to their community of faith. It is through these connections that people begin to have the sense that this is "their" church. The back door can never be completely closed, but it can be radically reduced in size.

DEVELOP A MINISTRY FLOW SYSTEM

This intentional strategy should be built around some type of "ministry flow" system. One of the most well-known flow systems is the baseball diamond made popular by Saddleback Community Church. If you are not aware of this, you can get the details in *The Purpose Driven Church* authored by Pastor Rick Warren. The basic principle of any flow system is that it effectively moves people who are disconnected from the church into connected community. Here are a few guidelines for developing such a system.

1. Keep It Simple

People engage more easily in that which they can understand. Do all you can to ensure that the flow system you design will allow people to know what to do, when to take the next steps, and where to go to engage in the system.

2. Adapt, Don't Adopt

Churches tend to want to adopt an existing system wholesale. The baseball diamond works well for Saddleback—but it must be remembered that it was designed for them specifically, not all churches generally. It provides a marvelous model, but you must still engage in the difficult work of contextualizing it to your unique setting. You may use a diamond, but each of your bases may be different. Or what it means to cross home plate in your system may be different from the one you adapted.

3. Make it Yours

The best way to make this point is to illustrate it. I met a young pastor who was determined to develop a ministry flow system. He liked the idea of showing progress, much like the ball diamond. However, he used a car racetrack for his diagram. Why? He lived in a community that is *big* into NASCAR. For his church, a track was more relevant than a diamond.

4. Believe it Enough to Own It

Do not develop a flow system just to have one. You must believe in it enough to implement it. Regardless of any criticism you may receive, work the system. If you do not believe it enough to own it, then either discard it or build one you can believe in.

CLOSE THE BACK DOOR, OR AT LEAST MAKE THE EXIT SMALLER

I was born and raised in San Diego, California. When I was growing up, the sports venue that housed both our professional baseball and football teams was Jack Murphy Stadium. This stadium seated in excess of 70,000 fans, with three decks that towered over the field-level seating. There were three methods one could use to get to the upper decks: elevator, escalator, or foot power. As a youngster, my favorite mode was walking—actually, running!

The designers of the stadium had developed an easy method of ambling up the several stories to the upper decks. There were no stairs; instead there were wide circular walkways. You entered these and simply followed them. Each cycle completed took you closer to the upper decks and eventually to the very top. At any point you could stop and rest. You also were able to peer over an inner rail and see the progress you had made.

Here are suggestions you might use to assimilate people into your church. Each one is a cycle made. They will provide a walkway for people to be connected more deeply into your community. In an ideal scenario, these would be implemented after a person has attended your church two or more times.

Identify any Invisible Fellowship Circles

Some churches have what Lyle Schaller calls an invisible "fellowship circle." This is a layer a person must penetrate to be genuinely "connected." It may not be intended, but if a person does not identify and negotiate these circles, he or she is held subtly at arm's length. Some potential invisible circles might be a small group, involvement in one-to-one discipleship, attending Sunday night church (yes, there are places this exists), involvement in Sunday school, sanctification, or speaking in tongues.

> The inability, or unwillingness, to find these invisible barriers will contribute greatly to inadequate assimilation.

The inability, or unwillingness, to find these invisible barriers will contribute greatly to inadequate assimilation. Do we want people to grow deeper and more connected? Absolutely! But we must diligently avoid the process becoming the very barrier it is intended to bridge: assimilation into a community of believers.

Send a Letter

Unlike the handwritten note suggested for initial follow-up, a letter to a repeat guest can be typewritten. It should come from the pastor, be personally signed, and be no more than one page in length. If the pastor personally met the person, a nice handwritten notation on the bottom would be advisable. A well-done information brochure should accompany the letter. Here are some suggestions for the letter's contents:

- Personal greeting (Dear _____ [fill in the name—not Dear Friend])
- Thank them for returning to the church
- Inform them of some key upcoming events
- Let them know the church is available for them if needed
- Encourage them in their week
- Invite them to return

Drop by with a Gift

Have teams of two do a "drop-by" visit. "Drop-by" means exactly that: They are dropping by. They will not call ahead, nor will they actually go inside the house or apartment (unless those being visited insist—and even at that, keep it less than fifteen minutes). It is suggested this visit be on the Saturday following the second visit—no earlier than 10 a.m. and no later than noon. The purpose is to show the church cares enough to make a special effort.

The gift needs to be something nonperishable and if food, not homemade. The folks being visited do not know your people well, so a homemade food item will probably find its way to the nearest trashcan. A nice basket with a few store-bought items, plus information about the church would be great. Include a card, letting them know the basket is from the church and the names of those who left it. There should also be an invitation for them to return.

This drop-by visit should take less than three minutes. Here is a possible scenario:

- The team knocks on the door.
- The door is answered.

- The drop-by team introduces themselves, telling the residents the team is from the church. They don't want to come in but wanted to give them this gift and thank them for being their guest. They also invite them to come again.
- They hand them the basket, thank them for their time, and encourage them to enjoy their Saturday.

If the drop-by team finds nobody at home, they simply leave the gift basket by the front door, but out of sight from the street (in case the people are out of town).

> Doing something is preferable to doing nothing; doing the right thing is more preferable to doing just anything.

Here, again, each church needs to know its community. The idea of an unannounced drop-by may be perceived as too pushy or disarming. If this is the case then you will need to determine what fits your context for follow up. The underlying principle is that a deeper level of contact must be initiated by the church. What is done is not nearly as important as something being done.

Make a Follow-up Phone Call

One of the members of the drop-by team will need to call

those who were visited. This call should be made late afternoon or early evening of the day they visited. If they talked to the folks, thank them again for their time and let them know they hope to see them the next day at church. If no one was at home, let them know you dropped by and left a gift by their front door. You want to make sure they found it.

Two final thoughts. First, make sure those who visit homes make a special effort to look for those individuals on the following Sunday. If the guests return and go unnoticed by those who came by their house, you will ensure them perceiving you as inauthentic. Second, voice mail systems count. When you make the post-visit phone call, connecting via a message on their answering system is acceptable (and in many cases preferable).

Implement a Flow System to Follow Them Through

A person and/or family who attends your church a third time must have an opportunity to flow into deeper church involvement. This system must fit your community and the personality of your church. The diagram you use (baseball diamond, racetrack, mountain to climb, stairs to walk up) makes no difference just as long as it makes a difference for you. Here are elements that should be considered for your flow system. As you review them, keep the following in mind: (1) They are not in any particular order; (2) they are not all inclusive; (3) they are flexible—feel free to use some, none, or all of them; and (4) they are fluid—add any of your own you feel are necessary for effective assimilation.

- *Introductory connection point:* People who are new to a community need a place to connect with others who are new. This could be something like a dessert event with the pastor(s) or a class designed to introduce them to the church's philosophy of ministry and how they can get involved. This type of newcomer's event or class could be a one-time gathering or spread over two to four weeks. One key is to provide it consistently.

- *Smaller cluster connections:* The goal is getting people from the large worship gathering into smaller groups. This could be Sunday school, cell groups, home groups, missions trips, sports teams, and so forth.

- *Authentication of connection to Christ:* People need to have the opportunity to understand their spiritual journey. They need to be able to know that they know they are in *relationship* with Christ. This could be through one-to-one appointments, a basic Christianity class, or an explore-your-faith experience. Whatever delivery system is used must be one that helps them affirm their born-again life and know their place in God's salvation story through Jesus.

- *Baptism:* People need to publicly declare their commitment to Christ. Baptism is a critical biblical mandate to do this. Give people regular opportunities for baptism, and make sure they understand what it means. Have them share their conversion stories via video or in person.

- *Deeper commitment (membership):* Deeper commitment to the community of believers needs to be part of your flow system. This is membership, however you define it. When conducting this aspect of assimilation, include the following: clear expectations of membership, public declaration of membership, and accountability in membership. Many churches are beginning to have folks renew their membership commitments yearly.

- *Ministry involvement:* People who have ownership will remain, and ownership happens through ministry involvement. Have all kinds of ministry opportunities. Make it a goal that all ministry happens in teams.

THE EXIT INTERVIEW

A church in northern California in an attempt to identify their invisible fellowship circle and develop their flow system conducted exit interviews. They identified five to seven families that had attended their church for three or more weeks, but then elected to move on. They contacted each family and discovered the following insights: The church was "very friendly," but somewhat impenetrable. The guests mentioned that they were greeted warmly, but those who welcomed them turned back to their circle of friends. The church also discovered that the ways to get involved were not outlined very well.

The leadership of this church is using this information to dramatically change their atmosphere and how they communicate new opportunities. If you choose to use an exit interview as part of your discovery process, these tips will be helpful:

- Determine the group you want to interview.
- Develop good questions.
- Decide who will make the calls.
- Don't be defensive at the answers.
- Design a strategy to address what you find.

When I was in Sunday school I learned a little ditty that probably every kid who attended Sunday school in the fifties and sixties learned. We would fold our hands with fingers interlaced in toward our palms. We then would be led in these words: "Here is the church, here is the steeple [we would extend our index fingers upward to make a steeple], open the doors and see all the people [at which time we would turn our hands over exposing our palms and interlaced fingers]." If only seeing all the people were that easy! If we don't work at narrowing our back door, we risk opening the door and wondering, *Where are all the people?*

KEY POINTS

1. Flow System
- Keep it simple.
- Adapt, don't adopt.
- Make it yours.
- Believe it enough to own it.

2. Elements of a Flow System
- Introductory connection point
- Smaller cluster connections
- Authentication of connection to Christ
- Baptism
- Deeper commitment (membership)
- Ministry involvement

DISCUSSION QUESTIONS

1. What are you currently doing to assimilate guests?

2. What are you using to determine its effectiveness?

3. What might you change to assimilate others more effectively?

4. What are you using to move people into deeper connection in your church?

ACTION STEPS

1. Review the suggestions made regarding assimilation. Which are you currently doing? Which do you feel you can implement?

2. Discuss the elements of the flow system. Describe your existing flow system. Evaluate and alter your flow system as necessary to make it more effective.

RESOURCES

- Gary McIntosh—*Beyond the First Visit*
- Rick Warren—*The Purpose Driven Church*
- Christian Swartz—*Natural Church Development*
- Thom Rainer, Eric Geiger—*Simple Church*

4 GET PEOPLE TO GROW

I was born and raised in Southern California, so seasonal change meant little to me. It was a bit cooler in the winter. A few trees changed colors in the fall. Spring brought a nice respite from the various rainy days we encountered. But, for the most part, I really didn't grasp the power of spring. Flowers still bloomed in the winter and people still mowed their lawns (although not as much), so the newness and freshness of spring was more conceptual than experiential.

Then something happened: I relocated to Indianapolis. Now spring makes perfect sense. The air warms, lawns turn from brown to green, flowers and trees begin to bud and blossom. This is the spring I had heard about. This is the spring that elicits enthusiasm and hope.

With my experiential discovery of spring came the realization of the requirements of spring. This new life needed to be nurtured. Flowers needed to be planted or replanted. Mulch had to be applied in the right quantities in the right places. The lawn equipment needed to be prepped. Watering had to be done. The new life spring brings may be a gift, but the nurturing of that gift requires work.

The same is true for believers. The new life a relationship with Christ provides must be nurtured. This nurturing demands intentional effort and energy. This brings us to the fourth question: *What are you doing to get people to grow?* This is a "discipleship" question.

Many churches do an excellent job of winning people to Christ and connecting them to the church, but do little to grow them in their faith. And there is a huge difference between being connected to a church and being a fully devoted follower of Christ.

> Superficiality is the curse of our age.
> — Richard Foster

When answering the discipleship question there are several assumptions to keep in mind:

1. *Discipleship is a process*. A person is not discipled as much as he or she is *being* discipled. Discipleship is

a lifelong journey that combines both personal initiative and community involvement.

2. *Discipleship is connective.* Genuine discipleship will strive to connect belief with behavior. "Those who say they live in God should live their lives as Jesus did" (1 John 2:6). Discipleship is helping followers of God live so their actions reflect their affirmations; their conduct matches their confession; who they say they are and who they are fit.

3. *Discipleship is all-encompassing.* Discipleship addresses each area of the believer's life. The Spiritual Formation Department of The Wesleyan Church states it this way: "To follow the Lord fully we must focus on the head (intellect and devotion), the heart (power and emotion) and the hand (intentional service)."

> A genuine disciple is a lifetime in the making.

Richard Foster has said, "Superficiality is the curse of our age." Asking and answering the discipleship question allows us to dig below the surface and combat superficial faith. It is not enough that we attract people to our churches. We must make our goal to develop them into fully devoted followers of Christ. We need to build people who will know what they believe and believe what they know. We need a mobilized people—people who act on what they know and believe. A discipleship that is passive (knowledge based only) will lose its power. A discipleship that is proactive (engaging people in their world) will demand power.

BUILDING A DISCIPLESHIP STRATEGY

You may have heard the phrase "We are building the boat as we go." I am not exactly sure what this means, except it has something to do with figuring things out as they're happening. This is fine—unless you are in the open ocean and need the boat. The flip side of this is that such can work out well as long as you keep the end result in your sights: You are building a boat.

This is how many churches approach discipleship. They simply figure it out as they go. The challenge with this approach is we are in the open ocean of spiritual need with our people. We need a boat now! We need to build it prior to launching out. We need to have a clear picture of the boat. Discipleship is the boat we are building. And we need to do all we can to ensure we have the proper material and blueprint. We need to keep the following in mind as we strive to help people to grow.

> Make the decision once . . . manage it daily.
>
> John Maxwell

Make the Choice

We read in Daniel 1:8, "But Daniel was determined . . ." We need to determine, to make up our minds, to build disciples. The commitment to grow is not a one-time venture, but a daily event. We choose the course, but we must consistently stay the course.

Know Your End Result

Discipleship is a process, but it is a process with an end in mind. Too often discipleship is merely an activity! We are busy "discipling," but have little understanding of the outcome we want in the lives of people. Discipleship should result in change. But what change? Knowing this is central to achieving the desired end result. We need to have an awareness of the change we are looking for in those we help to mature in the faith.

I have had the privilege of staying at a five-star hotel. I was very impressed with the service I received and assumed a hotel was either five-star at its inception or it wasn't. What I discovered is that hotels earn their five-star rating.

An article in *USA Today* titled "How They Rate" provided the checklist the Mobil Travel Guide uses to qualify hotels for the highest rating. This checklist included the following:

- Bags should arrive in the room within ten minutes of check-in.
- Wake-up calls should be delivered by a person, not a machine.
- Room service should be delivered within thirty minutes of ordering at a hotel, forty at a resort.
- At breakfast in the restaurant, coffee cups should never be empty for more than thirty seconds.
- Employees should use the guest's name when interacting.

This is a wonderful example of knowing the end result. The qualifications for a five-star rating have been determined, and knowing them allows hotels to implement the necessary systems to achieve this desired result. The same should be true for churches. They need to know what they want to see reflected in the lives of people, so that they can design a discipleship process to achieve those ends.

Model True Discipleship

Discipleship is not a "do as I say, not as I do" venture. We must be able to say with Paul, "And you should imitate me, just as I imitate Christ" (1 Cor. 11:1). Steve Sjogren challenges us with these words: "It's a simple but unalterable truth: Your people become the sort of disciple you embody and present to them as a model."

Discipleship begins with the leader. What kind of Jesus follower are you? What is God doing in your life that you would like to see reproduced in the lives of those you lead? Good, bad, or indifferent—your church will reflect you. If you have led your church for more than three years, what you see is primarily your reflection. Take an honest look at the people you lead. Determine to lead them in a way that will stretch them and you.

Provide Helpful Resources

It has been said that if you don't know where you are going, any road will do. This is often the case with the material we use for discipleship. When we don't know our end result, we tend to gravitate toward the best "packaged" stuff; if it looks good, it must be good. When we know where we want to lead our people, we will look with intention. We will find materials that move us toward our destination.

I suggest the following considerations when looking for a discipleship resource:

- Be sure it is grounded in Scripture.
- Run denominational material through the same filter you would any other.
- Avoid reinventing the wheel.
- Adapt the material as needed.
- Be aware of theological distinctives.

Promote Active Discipleship

A discipleship that only intersects the head and does not extend through the heart and into the hands will be only partially effective. It may increase knowledge, but it will never rally people to missional engagement. Too often the emphasis has been on "knowing" not "doing." Christ's command to his disciples was to *go* not *know*. It was to "go and make," not "know and make."

Discipleship has become a program to instill understanding of Scripture instead of a process encouraging the utilization of Scripture in daily life. Genuine disciples get into life. They connect with those disengaged from God. They have pure hearts and dirty hands. An active discipleship program fuels this. There is a biblical foundation from which Christ followers work, but it is conviction of the

> Produce disciples who do stuff, not just know stuff.
> — Steve Sjogren

clarity of their mission that forces them into ministry involvement.

An active discipleship program is balanced. It encourages the head (knowledge), it enables the heart (experiential), and it equips the hands (ministry). When these all interconnect, each person will become more like Jesus. When the true power of the Holy Spirit joins with our heads, hearts and hands—the whole of Christ and genuine personal holiness is made visible through the Church by and for every generation.

Build by Multiplication

Paul said to Timothy, "You have heard me teach many things that have been confirmed by many reliable witnesses. Now teach these truths to other trustworthy people who will be able to pass them on to others" (2 Tim. 2:2). Excellent discipleship is not about one person being discipled, but discipleship multiplication. Discipleship ought to be reproducible. In fact, a Christian cannot be complete until he or she is investing in others.

When my daughter, Megan, was seven or eight she took six baton lessons through the local parks and recreation department. At the completion of those six lessons she knew how to "kinda" twirl a baton.

She did not know all that much about the art of "batoning," but she did know she knew more than the neighbor girl who had never had a lesson. What did she do? She promptly recruited the neighbor girl into *her* baton class for one dollar a lesson. Megan only had six lessons, but what she knew she was determined to pass on to others.

This same attitude needs to be incorporated into a discipleship plan. Part of the process should be sharing what you have learned with others. It should incorporate taking people along in ministry arenas. It needs to offer opportunities for people to learn by doing and experimenting. If Paul hadn't poured into Timothy, and Timothy into others, and those others into others, the Church would have lasted a mere generation. Multiplication is the lifeblood of the Church!

EVALUATE EFFECTIVENESS REGULARLY

Regularly evaluate the discipleship method and material you use. Local churches tend to begin something and allow it to run unchecked, never revisiting it to determine its ongoing effectiveness in regard to its intended purpose. The dynamics of your church change, the leading of the Spirit redirects, spiritual maturity levels ebb and flow.

Each of these contributes to the necessity for regular evaluation.

Effective evaluation is based on two components. First, *know what you are evaluating.* This has to do with the desired results. If you have only a vague idea as to where you are going, you will not be able to adequately measure the effectiveness of the vehicle you are using to get there. Second, *define success.* Success is a moving target. It may never be hit unless clearly defined. Most people would define a successful fishing trip as catching fish. But this may not be an adequate definition. John van Vliet, in his article "3 Fishing Trips You Have to Take," defines it this way: "You count your success not in the number of fish caught, but in the fact that you spent a day without your cell phone and you never missed it."

What are you evaluating? What is success? Answering these two questions will contribute greatly to designing an effective discipleship.

Discipleship is a critical element of your church's being missional. When authentic disciples are made, they are engaged with the mandate to go! Robert Coleman says, ". . . the Great Commission as a life-style [encompasses] the total resources of every child of God." It is this Great Commission lifestyle that discipleship should address. A discipleship that has as its desired outcome "to produce better members" is extremely shortsighted. A discipleship that embraces the challenge to make Great Commission followers of Christ will reap an unprecedented harvest. For it is these disciples who will view all of their life as the mission field they have been sent to cultivate. This is the kind of disciples you will want to build.

KEY POINTS
- Discipleship is a process—connective and all-encompassing.
- The building blocks of discipleship are as follows:
  (1) make the decision; (2) know the end result;
  (3) model true discipleship; (4) provide helpful resources;
  (5) promote active discipleship; (6) build by multiplication.

DISCUSSION QUESTIONS

1. What in your life reflects the kind of disciples you want to produce?

2. How will you integrate this into your discipleship program?

3. What things in your life do you not want reflected in the disciples you want to produce?

4. What changes will you make?

ACTION STEPS

Describe your current discipling process.

Describe your dream disciple.

What is the desired result of your discipleship process?

Have you been achieving this result?

When was the last time you evaluated discipleship effectiveness?

RESOURCES
- Robert E. Coleman—*The Master Plan of Discipleship*
- Wayne Cordeiro—*Doing Church as a Team*
- Bill and Lynne Hybels—*Rediscovering Church*

5 GET PEOPLE TO GO

The prayer had to be said—words were not enough. Jesus was soon to be arrested, tried, abandoned, crucified, buried, and, eventually, resurrected. But what He had shared was too much. His disciples may have *thought* they understood what He was sharing (John 16:16–28). They told Him so when they declared, "Now we understand . . ." (John 16:30). But He knew they really did not understand. How could they? They were about to enter one of the darkest times of their lives.

They would see Him dead on a cross, and the harshness of His death would extinguish their hope like a bucket of water poured on a lit match. And once hope departs, discouragement, disengagement, and disinterest are not far behind. It would have been easy for the disciples to compromise on their call. The words they claimed to have understood would be lost in the hollowness of Jesus' death. They needed His prayer—a prayer that would empower them once the realization of His resurrection shattered the reality of His death. They would need to be reminded that they were a missionary people because He was a missionary Savior.

The prayer of Jesus, recorded by John in the seventeenth chapter of his gospel, clarifies missional ministry. In this prayer of commissioning, Jesus vividly portrays the missional aspect of ministry: His, the disciples', and ours.

THE MISSIONAL MINISTRY OF JESUS

God gave (sent) His Son into the world out of His love for the world (John 3:16–17). God did this out of a heart of salvation, not condemnation. Jesus undergirds this in His prayer when He declares, "And this is the way to have eternal life—to know you, the only true God, and Jesus Christ, the one you *sent* to earth" (John 17:3, emphasis added). Jesus makes clear that the strength of His followers is that they understood He had been sent. "Now they know that everything I have is a gift from you, for I have passed on to them the message you gave me. They accepted it and know that I came from you, and they believe you *sent* me" (verses 7–8, emphasis added).

THE MISSIONAL MINISTRY OF THE DISCIPLES

Jesus' physical ministry on the earth was limited to a three-year span. He was going to depart, leaving the disciples behind (John 17:11). They would now need to take up the "sent" mantle. They are not to be taken out of the world (verse 15), but sent into the world as Jesus modeled for them. "Just as you *sent* me into the world, I am *sending* them into the world" (verse 18, emphasis added). Being sent, going out, is central to the ministry of those who follow Christ. It is an extension of His being sent by the Father into the world.

THE MISSIONAL MINISTRY OF THE TWENTY-FIRST CENTURY

He extends the same ministry to us today. The same prayer He prayed for His followers in the first century He prayed for us: "I am praying not only for these disciples but also for all who will ever believe in me through their message" (John 17:20). We are part of the "all who will ever believe" because of our acceptance of the message. Our decision to believe should result in the same "sentness" as the first disciples'. The time distance between us and the death and resurrection of Jesus does not negate the commission of being sent out.

The church has lost this missional mentality. We have forgotten it is not about people coming to us, but our going to people. When we fully engage in being sent, we extend the ministry for which Jesus prayed. It is in our going that we fulfill His desire for our lives. In a sense, it is in our "sentness" that we are an answer to Jesus' prayer.

"I pray that they will all be one, just as you and I are one—as you are in me, Father, and I am in you. And may they be in us so that the world will believe you *sent* me" (John 17:21, emphasis added).

"I am in them and you are in me. May they experience such perfect unity that the world will know that you *sent* me and that you love them as much as you love me" (John 17:23, emphasis added).

> It is in our "sentness" that we are an answer to Jesus' prayer.

"O righteous Father, the world doesn't know you, but I do; and these disciples know you *sent* me" (John 17:25, emphasis added).

It is clear that when we respond to our missional call, the world catches glimpses of Jesus. The Church's willingness to engage the world *in* the world is a singular clarion call to the reality of God! People best see God and engage with God when His Church is going out.

When the Church acts on its "sentness," salvation is not an ending, but a radical beginning. When we stop at *our* salvation, we negate our heartfelt gratitude. It is out of that gratitude our call to serve springs. Service is more than an activity we engage in; it is a responsibility into which we must immerse ourselves. Service is the tangible living out of being sent.

What are you doing to get your people to go is a question that helps a local body engage its culture. This is a "missional" question, one that results in the church wrestling with the prayer of John 17. A church that has as its emphasis a desire to *grow* apart from the willingness to *go* is not living as Jesus intended. We are foremost a missionary people. Emil Brunner has said, "A church exists by mission as fire exists by burning." Let's be a burning church!

ATTRACTIONAL OR MISSIONAL?

In Sacramento County (where I used to live) one community, Arden-Arcade, wanted to incorporate and become its own city. One of the driving forces behind this was that they were paying out $33 million but only getting back $20 million in services.

In response to this, Roger Dickinson, a county supervisor said, "The argument that 'we should get back everything we generate' is fundamentally an argument that 'we don't have a responsibility.' That's a very troubling argument to me."

Unfortunately, this is the attitude of many churches. All that is generated is expected to serve their ends. Ministry is defined as what happens on their property. Community involvement is limited to what they can do for the community at their facility. Seldom is thought given to going out into the community. This is what is known as an "attractional" church.

An attractional church is a "come and see" church. Their ministry tends to center around getting people from the community onto their property—or into their church—to see what they have to offer. The primary motivation is getting people in the door. Characteristics of an attractional church are as follows:

- The church functions primarily as a purveyor of religious goods and services.
- The primary task of the church is to bring people from the culture into the church to participate in their programs.
- It prioritizes its resources (time, energy, and money) inward.
- The focus is on getting people to "come and see" what they are doing.
- Everything is designed to enhance the building, increase attendance, and gain members.

This kind of church is missing the "sent" nature of its ministry. This is not the kind of church Jesus prayed for in John 17. Jesus prayed for a missional church. A church that is sent! A church that takes seriously Christ's command to "go and make disciples of all the nations" (Matt. 28:19).

What is a missional church? The missional church is a "go and be" community. Milfred Minatrea, in *Shaped by God's Heart*, states that "a missional church expresses the incarnational reality of Christ, present and ministering in the world." A missional church takes seriously its "sent" commission. It looks outward. It views attraction as being Christ in the world. There is an awareness that the world will know the Heavenly Father when His earthly kids get intentional about not being constrained by church property lines. Here are some characteristics of a missional church:

- The primary task of the church is sending people out of the church into the culture.
- People are sent as missionaries within their own culture.
- This is a church that sees its role as getting people in not to keep them, but to send them.
- A missional church multiplies believers, leaders, and churches.
- Home-based ministries are strengthened to provide a hub of sending activity.

A missional church is not anti-attraction. It can't be if it takes to heart its "sent" commission. The motivation to attract, however, is much different. A missional church *brings* people in to *build* people up to *send* people out.

A missional church invests beyond itself, recognizing that the scoring system is much more than measuring what happens on the property. "Keeping score" is not the issue. We do, and should, keep score. What changes is the scoring system. Church becomes a seven-days-a-week activity, not just one hour on Sunday morning.

Once the score is understood, then the necessary steps can be taken to be effective in the scoring system. A church that determines to ask this question of mission is moving from programs to process, models to mission, attraction to incarnation, seating to sending, and decisions to disciples. A church must be intentional about moving from attraction alone to being missionally motivated. It is a decision that is made by the leadership. Seldom does a church stumble into mission.

MOVING FROM ATTRACTION TO MISSION

Put an Emphasis on Members as Missionaries

> The church is one of the few organizations in the world that does not exist for the benefit of its members.
> Ed Stetzer

In recent years local churches have ramped up their membership expectations. Membership has become a statement of higher commitment, not merely increased privilege. That said, why would "membership" in the Kingdom be any less demanding than membership in a high-expectation church?

Believers will never be effectively mobilized apart from a deep sense of service. Salvation is both personal (saved from our sin) and communal (saved to engage in purposeful service). This salvation results in active participation in the mission of responding to our "sentness."

We are saved to be a missionary people. The church is to equip its people for this saving purpose. This equipping is about three things: community, spirituality, and mission. Each is separate, but they are intimately connected in their role of mobilization.

The challenge is balance. Salvation can be, selfishly, an end point; but service can also be misconstrued as the only indicator of our salvation. Salvation is not just for us, but for others; yet we must not forget it is for us! However, our salvation is best lived out for us in our service for others. God saves us personally so we might serve publicly.

This is the emphasis the community of believers must place on membership. Members are to be missionaries in their world. A "missionary" is not defined as someone who ventures cross-culturally or overseas, but as anyone who boldly engages his or her world in purposeful living.

Teach on Missional Living

Teaching on missional living naturally flows from a commitment to emphasize members as missionaries. Missionaries are not sent ill-equipped. A new approach must be taken to teaching those in your community of faith. Cultural awareness must be heightened. Believers must be encouraged and taught to look at their neighborhoods, workplaces, and communities with the eyes of a missionary.

In their book *Breaking the Missional Code* Stezter and Putman share many insights on teaching missional living. I will share four as a baseline.

- *Fall in love with people*. If the church does not genuinely care about the community that surrounds it, there will be no motivation to invest in it. Too often churches become a Gilligan's Island—they have their own culture, while the world has changed around them.

- *Die to yourself and your preferences.* It is not about what we like, but what will best connect with the folks in the community we have been called to reach. My wife and I have committed to being part of a core team for a new church. We have had to remind ourselves regularly it is not what we prefer, but what we will need to do to reach those in our mission field.

- *Do prayer walks.* This is simply taking the time to walk or drive the community and pray. Ask God to open your eyes to the needs of those in the homes you pass. Ask God to guide your prayers. Out of these impressed prayer needs you will begin to discern what you might do to connect people to Christ.
- *Understand where God is working in churches and in cultures.* God is at work. We need to find out where the work is being done and join God there. Help the people in your church to pay attention to the opportunities God is creating in their neighborhoods, workplaces, and families.

Empower People to Engage Culture

The first church I pastored was in Southern California. Ken was a member of the church. He loved sports, and he oversaw the athletic ministry. When I arrived we had a softball team and basketball team, both of which participated in church leagues. He was well connected to city softball leagues. He umpired for many years and competed on city teams.

One day we were chatting, and he shared his heart to use sports to reach men and women in the city. I looked him in the eye and said, "Ken, God wants to use you to do just that. I will do all I can to help you." Tears welled up in the eyes of this bear of a man, and at that point he felt a release to engage the sports culture of our city.

God honored his heart. We grew from one softball and basketball team competing in church leagues to five softball teams (men's, women's, and coed), two coed volleyball teams, and one basketball team. Most of the teams were in the city league and were populated by unchurched people. Many came to Christ as a result of those teams.

What happened? Ken was released to engage his culture, the culture of city sports. He was freed to engage people where they were, with a method that could connect with them. People played on a church team, but did not have to attend the church; yet many began to attend. People played on a church team, but did not have to confess Christ as Lord; yet many did just that. A church with a missional approach does ministry to connect with people, not simply connect them to church.

When a church applauds just as loudly those who serve outside the church as they do inside the church, it is moving toward a missional mind-set. When a church encourages as "real" ministry people coaching sports teams or serving on community boards and neighborhood groups as much, if not more, as serving on church related work, it is moving toward a missional mind-set. When the pastor understands the limited time resources of her or his people and suggests they pick community involvement over church-only participation, he or she is moving toward a missional mind-set.

Downplay Involvement in Church-Only Activities

To mobilize your people for mission you must release them to be in their culture. A church that keeps their people too busy with "church activities" will effectively remove them from the culture they are to engage. Affirm involvement in community activities, even when it might conflict with attending a church event. Let people know serving on a city board is just as much a ministry as serving on a church board. If you have so many church activities that your people have no time or energy to be with their neighbors, you may have too many activities.

Place a High Value on Church Planting

A church that is committed to getting people to go will value church planting. Church planting is a marvelous way of asking your people to go! New churches are in desperate need of core members to help establish a base for effective ministry. Existing churches are populated with potential core members.

A pastor must give people permission to go. A missional church will gladly allow their people the permission and opportunity to go and help begin a new church. Talk about church planting. Invite church planters to share with your people. Challenge your people to be open to God's call of helping start new churches.

Determine to Be a Transformational Community

> Without regard to locations, missional churches are actively releasing members to new ministries and new churches. Their passion is to see the churches grasp the principles of multiplication.
> Rich Rusaw

Transformation can only happen up close and personal. Yeast transforms dough when it is intermingled with it, not simply set beside it. A church will only be able to transform others when they intermingle.

Churches believe that if they have a piece of property or a building, they are present in the community. This is a mistake. A church's presence in a community is not its building or its property but its involvement in the life of the community. A church that views its building as a home for the saints, instead of a hub for ministry training, will eventually be rendered useless.

Passing through a small town in rural Wisconsin, I noticed that a church building had become, literally, a museum. It had "museum" written above the entrance. I have no idea the history of that town or that church, but it struck me that this will be the fate of many existing churches if they lose their missional base.

Determine to be transformational. Decide to move out beyond the walls of your church into the center of your culture. Only a transformational community will stir people to want to believe.

KEY POINTS

1. An Attractional Church
    - Is a purveyor of religious goods and services
    - Brings people from the culture into the church
    - Prioritizes resources inward
    - Gets people to "come and see"
    - Enhances building, increases attendance, and gains members
2. A Missional Church
    - Sends people into the culture
    - Views people as missionaries to their culture
    - Gets people in to send out
    - Multiplies believers, leaders, and churches
    - Is a hub of sending activity

DISCUSSION QUESTIONS

1. How do you understand Jesus' prayer in John 17?

2. How do we live missionally in the world?

3. How might we become selfish in our salvation?

4. What might we do to live out our "sentness"?

ACTION STEPS

1. Develop a prayer-walk strategy for your community.

2. Review the characteristics of a "come and see" church and a "go and be" church. Which is most descriptive of your church? Why?

3. Review the six steps to being more missional. Discuss how your church currently measures up.

4. Honestly answer this question: What can we do in our community, for our community, that if we were no longer here would cause us to be missed?

RESOURCES

- Ed Stetzer—*Planting Missional Churches*
- Alan J. Roxburgh, Fred Romanuk—*The Missional Leader*
- Erwin McManus—*An Unstoppable Force*
- Phil Stevenson—*The Ripple Church*
- Rick Rusaw, Eric Swanson—*The Externally Focused Church*

APPENDIX

SEEING YOUR COMMUNITY THROUGH MISSIONAL EYES

Use this worksheet as a guide. It may not be possible to answer every item, but answer those that you can.

1. Describe who and what you see, feel, hear on your way to church and back home. Drive a different route(s) to church. Is there anything different?

2. Become acquainted with the community as intimately as possible.

a. Walk the community. Walk through the community, absorbing all the sights, sounds, aromas. It is better to walk than to use a car. The community can be divided up, and people can be assigned to walk certain areas. Also, several people can walk the same area together, with each paying attention to a particular assigned perspective

b. Assign people to hold conversations with a variety of community residents, church leaders from other churches in the community, civic leaders, and business people. Ask them what they think are the pressing needs not being met at present—or being met inadequately.

c. Survey neighbors about pressing needs and how your church could be a help to the community. In a survey you can ask if people currently attend any Christian congregation or group in the community. If the answer is no, make sure their names and addresses are collected for follow-up. Additionally, you can inform people surveyed of ministries offered by your church and others.

d. Collect statistical data from sources such as the 2000 Census, government agencies (city planning, school district, county), chamber of commerce, and land use plans. Use the information to do the following:

- Determine the percentage of ethnic groups.
- Determine age distribution, income levels, family patterns, housing patterns, and educational levels.
- Identify the public schools that are located in the community, and determine their characteristics.
- Identify daycare centers and/or nursery schools in the community.
- Identify the healthcare facilities in the community.
- Identify the recreation facilities/programs in the community.
- Identify the community organizations and social service organizations in the community.
- Are there changes since the 2000 census data? If so, what? Were there surprises in the data?

Note: Although gathering census data is important, place more emphasis on getting to know your neighbors through conversation and fellowship than on census data alone.

   e. Determine the ministries that are being carried out by churches in the community.

f. Explore information about the future of the area.

3. Determine the strength and the needs of the community.

a. Interpret the collected data described in Step 2. Catalogue the community needs from interviews, and compare these needs with the ministries that are being carried out by churches in the community. On the basis of what has been learned, what conclusions can be drawn regarding the needs of the community? What possibilities for ministries can you envision as you look at this data?

b. Place emphasis on the resources and potential all ready present in the community.

c. Identify the greatest unmet needs, whether physical/economic, intellectual/emotional, social/political, or spiritual.

4. Study your own congregation.

a. Examine your church's history and its recent past in order to look toward the future.

b. Determine what the dimensions of the current mission and ministry of the church are. Is there an adopted mission statement?

c. Determine what programming is offered and who is participating.

d. Determine the impact right now of the church in the community. Determine the images that church members have of the community and, conversely, how the community views the church.

e. Determine what resources of any type are available for expanded ministry. Talk to members of the congregation. Ask what specific human hurts and hopes they long to help with.

f. Determine what the strengths and lesser strengths are of the congregation and its facility.